A PILLAR OF STRENGTH

Memoir of
Geetha Balasubramanian

by
Dr. Uma Balasubramaniam

as told to
Rohini S. Murthy

NEEMTREE
Publishing House

A PILLAR OF STRENGTH
A Memoir of Geetha Balasubramanian

Neemtree Publishing House
Phone : +91 8550931939
contact@neemtreelabs.com
First published on 15th Jan 2026

Author : Dr. Uma Balasubramaniam

Cover : Girish Sahastrabudhe

Layout : Arvind AartiVishnu Rajandekar

Printed by : Square Digital
Near Perugate, Sadashiv Peth, Pune 411030
Phone – 020 - 24459954

ISBN : 978-81-990432-7-5

I dedicate this to my parents,

my husband, and

my children

for their unwavering support.

~

INDEX

FOREWORD

They say that God could not be everywhere, and so he created mothers. But have we ever wondered how it feels to be cared for by God himself? You feel protected from every storm, loved unconditionally and supported with the quiet confidence that you can achieve anything in life.

This is exactly what we experienced in the love and presence of our beloved mother. Her role in our life was not limited to being just a parent- she was our mentor, our teacher, and our moral compass. Every decision she made and every action she took became a lesson for us. Today, our abilities, our values, our attitude, and even the way we look at the world are shaped by her wisdom, her discipline, and her unwavering sense of purpose.

Uma, our eldest sister, has always been the ideal daughter- steadfast, gentle, caring, and deeply devoted. As a sister, she has been our constant source of support, strength, and affection. When she came up with the idea of writing a book, I silently thought that she is probably the most uniquely qualified person to narrate the life journey of our mother and to illuminate the grit and quiet brilliance with which she lived.

Without diverting from facts or hinging on exaggeration, Uma has vividly depicted the unparalleled goodness of our mother which positively impacted many lives she touched. As you read through these concise yet rousing story, you will realize that our mother's life is not merely a story but an inspiration. It is a reminder of the power of character, the depth of a mother's love, and the legacy that lives on long after the person has left this world.

Vijay Balasubramaniam - *brother*
B.E,PMP
Senior Director- L&T Mindtree

FOREWORD

My mum was simple, straightforward and pretty. All this is completely true but I am extremely grateful for her complete focus and dedication in guiding her children towards a meaningful life. My list of 'thank you mum' is very lengthy as I can keep going on about how much she has done for us. However, I can only hope and pray that I am reborn as her loving daughter.

There are lots of fond memories with my mom. The most special ones include my mum taking us for ice creams and watching movies in the theatre. Once, we watched 2 shows back-to-back. In general, my siblings and I had great fun with her.

All the efforts she used to take in managing the household and working in RBI is truly praiseworthy. But these responsibilities never stopped her from having a great time.

I am glad that my sister Uma has written such a touching memoir of our mother. My mother's will power, positive thinking and many other amazing traits, which you will read in this book can become a great source of inspiration and strength.

Dr. Meenakshi Arun - *Sister.*

ACKNOWLEDGEMENT

I am deeply grateful to my father, my husband and my two children who encouraged me to pen this memoir. I extend my gratitude to my siblings -Vijay and his family and Meenakshi and her family .

I would like to thank my writer and publisher for their dedication and expertise in bringing this work to life. Your thoughtful suggestions and professionalism have enriched every page.

About Uma Balasubramanian

Dr. Uma Balasubramanian holds multiple qualifications including M.B.B.S, D.G.O, MRCOG, MRCGP, DFSRH, and a Postgraduate Certificate in Healthcare Leadership. Currently based in Norfolk, UK, she balances her career with family life alongside her husband, a consultant Orthopaedic Surgeon at Peterborough City Hospital, and their two children - Srivatsa, a medical student at Leicester Medical School, and Sneha, a year 12 student in Perse school Cambridge.

Dr. Uma is a GP Partner at Boughton Surgery in Kings Lynn and serves as Medical Education Lead for Fens and Brecks PCN. She also trains future GPs through the Kings Lynn VTS scheme. Previously, she held leadership roles including Assistant Medical Director at South Lincolnshire CCG and Prescribing Lead at West Norfolk CCG. She is also a medical tutor for Cambridge University medical students.

Beyond medicine, she enjoys cooking, music, dance, movies, and gardening. Being passionate about preserving her Indian heritage, she celebrates all festivals like Navratri and Diwali and teaches her children our rich Indian culture. Dr. Uma also embraces her culture through traditional activities like pujas and festivities.

Committed to giving back to the society, she has participated in charity walks, raising funds for Dementia and Parkinson's UK. Her dedication to medicine, education, culture, and community shapes her holistic approach to life and care.

■

About the Writer

Rohini S. Murthy is a freelance writer and a former Public Relations professional with 25 years of work experience. After obtaining a Master's degree in Mass Communication from Bangalore University, she started her career with a leading PR firm in Bangalore. To strike a work life balance, she opted to become a work from home professional in 2009. Her articles have appeared in leading publications like Deccan Herald, Indian Express, Hindustan Times, DNA, Filmfare etc. She has also ghost-written blogs, speeches, voice over scripts and website content for several corporates and individuals alike.

She holds the credit of editing the first comic book on menstrual health and hygiene called Moontime.In 2024, she authored a book titled Nadayogi Shankara, a biography of the Late Shri Bangalore Shankara Rao, a flutist par excellence.

She has also edited a book called Food Guru that enables readers understand their own body through Ayurvedic wisdom. Besides writing extensively on various topics, she is adept in social media management also.

Having once worked as a teacher to a blind student, she got inspired to take up social welfare activities, which she hopes to pursue in a consistent manner in the near future.

She can be reached on - shekarrohini@gmail.com

Geetha – Living the Gita's wisdom

When you hear the name Geetha.... What is the first thing that comes to your mind? The answer is quite obviously Bhagavad Gita! This sweet-sounding Sanskrit name means a sacred song or hymn. Gita also symbolizes musicality and spirituality, embodying beauty, wisdom, and devotional significance. I was quite amazed by the fact that my mother was an embodiment of all the traits her name signifies. This made me wonder whether my grandparents had a premonition of sorts that their little Geetha would grow up to be a woman who excelled in all her roles as a daughter, sister, wife, mother, friend, colleague, neighbour and also did her duty to the best of ability just like Lord Krishna said!

I remember, my mother would often remark that a grown-up person's behaviour or traits is reflective of their upbringing. As a mother of two (my son is an adult while my daughter is a teenager), I can vouch for her thought process now. As her daughter, I may sound a bit biased when I say that, 'Geetha was the best mother any child could hope for!' However, when I mentioned this to my cousins a couple of years ago about my mother being the best, they readily agreed. I was quite amazed and asked them, 'Oh so you agree that she is the best mother, I thought you would say your mother is the best'. Our conversation may sound silly but the fact that my cousins were in total agreement speaks volumes about my mother.

■

A Master Multitasker – Life Lessons for everyone

Nowadays, we often hear or read about work life balance. Though such terminology didn't exist back in the day, my mother never cribbed or fretted about managing home and office work. She dedicated her time and energy in equal measure and did so with a smile. In fact, many of her female colleagues would jokingly say, 'Madam, can you share some tips about how to be like you'.

Some people have their own unique way to strike a balance when it comes to home and work and my mother was one such person, who personified this. I may sound prejudiced while writing about my mother, but the fact remains that there are scores of people, outside our family who knew my mother well and wholeheartedly agree that she was an extraordinarily good human being and an incredible mother who literally dedicated her life to her 3 children and family.

Her children's education ranked supreme on her wish list. She constantly enquired about good schools, tuition teachers, and related options. Later in life, she even learnt astrology so that she could match horoscopes when her children reached marriageable age. Since all three of us had arranged marriages, her knowledge of astrology came in handy.

Investing in stocks and learning about the nitty-gritties of real estate was another passion that she put her heart and soul into. While her acumen in understanding the complex world of stocks strengthened our financial status, the surplus money she earned was skilfully directed towards buying land and apartments for her children.

My dear reader may wonder how one woman can possess so many skills? In fact, this is a question I would often ask her, "Mum, you work full time in RBI, you come home and start cooking for all of us and in free time over the weekend you get busy with stock market and real estate. How do you manage to do all this?". Her reply would be quite straightforward and simple, 'Uma, if you put your heart and soul into doing anything, then it ceases to feel stressful. In fact, you may start enjoying the process and that is what I do. I like being a working woman and at the same time, I love being a wife and mother too. When I want to pursue an interest or a hobby, I don't postpone it to another day. I begin to take small steps and that is how my passion towards the stock market and real estate has grown to this level.' Though she forgot to mention cooking as her passion, I must mention here that her culinary skills were exemplary. Even to this day, I fondly recollect her signature dish Avial. In fact, many of our friends in Delhi would come home to learn it from her. She would find great joy in trying out new recipes.

At work, her colleagues marvelled at her speed and accuracy, especially her quickness in performing math calculations.

Be it a colleague, vegetable vendor, house help, a shopkeeper or a neighbour, anyone who had a long association appreciated her ability to manage many roles with skill and dedication. In fact, they would often remark - 'I doubt if there can be another Geetha in this world'.

■

Speaking from the heart

She always spoke her mind. But after getting to know her, people would appreciate her straightforwardness and remark, 'we know she is not the kind who speaks one thing to our face and goes and says something else behind our back'. I feel this is a precious trait in today's world.

The genuineness of the person, someone who speaks without malice or a trace of ego is indeed a rare quality. My mother personified the fact that a person who speaks from the heart can appeal to people of all age groups.

I often say my mother was my first teacher, my quiet strength, and my greatest role model. Everything I am today has a trace of her, her voice, her patience, her discipline, and above all, her unshakable spirit.

So, join me as I open the gates of memory....

■

Roots of Resilience

My mother, Geetha, was born on April 7th, 1951, in Chennai. My grandfather, Mr. Doraisamy was a government employee while my grandmother Mrs.Indirani worked as an English teacher on and off. My mother's childhood unfolded like chapters in a moving book, each chapter beginning in a new city. My grandfather's job took the family from one city to another. From Hubli to Mysore and finally to Bangalore, she walked through different cultures and dialects. Each move placed her in different surroundings. Every new place meant a new school, new friends, and new beginnings. But instead of seeing it as a burden, she took it as an adventure. This constant shifting taught her how to adapt, how to start over, and how to stay calm no matter where life placed her.

She grew up in a middle-class home where values were sacred. Her grandmother, Visalakshi, and her father shaped her understanding of life - faith, honesty, and boldness became her foundation. She learned early that prayer wasn't just about asking, but about thanking. Dignity was not about status, but about integrity. She often told me about her grandmother and her strict and disciplined father - how their gentle teachings on respect, prayer, and dignity became the framework for the life she would build.

As a child, she dreamt of becoming a doctor. She was very good in her studies but circumstances prevented her from pursuing medicine. Many would have been crushed by this disappointment, but not my mother. She studied science, joined NCC as a cadet and then became an Under officer, and excelled in all the activities including rifle shooting. She was very patriotic to India and even when she was ill, she would salute the flag and sing the national anthem.

She loved music, especially old Hindi songs of Mohammed Rafi and Kishore Kumar. She also enjoyed watching movies and never missed an opportunity to learn and soak up knowledge in every form. Not someone to complain or crib, she just believed in moving forward. This ability to accept whatever came her way and make the best of it became her trademark strength and a motivation to family, friends and relatives. She had a lively spirit and a rare zest for life. Her gentle laughter and quick wit made every moment with her joyful.

■

Through Time & Trials – Their Journey together

My mom was barely 21 when my grandmother started insisting that she gets married as she was the eldest daughter. My mom had a younger brother and sister who were studying in a hostel at that point of time. My mom was young, very fair, beautiful, and working at RBI. She was the apple of her father's eye. She wanted to marry someone who was fair, good looking, and rich. But when alliances started coming, many of the proposals came with demands for dowry. My grandmother was quite astute and could not afford dowry as money was limited and moreover, she had to plan the education of her other two children.

My parents had an arranged marriage. Unlike my mother who had just 2 siblings, my father came from a large family with 6 siblings. His father i.e. my paternal grandfather was a teacher and my maternal grandmother was an English teacher. This common profession helped them to bond very well. The best part was my father's family never asked for dowry and so my grandmother was very keen that my mom marry him. But my father was very different from what my mom had dreamed. He was not fair and not rich, though their family owned a house and some lands. He was simple but not the handsome man she hoped for.

At the same time, there was another proposal from a young IAS officer who was very fair and rich. It was quite confusing as to which proposal to go for. Moreover, my mother's horoscope matched with both men, which made things all the more confusing. My grandmother was in a dilemma. My grandmother was a great devotee of Sai Baba and she prayed to Baba all her life. She went to meet her guru at the Thyagarajanagar Sai Baba temple in south Bangalore. She explained the situation to him. After lending a patient ear to her, Radhakrishna Swamiji simply said, 'Kannan will come and marry Geetha'. His reply stunned and confused her even further as neither of the boy's names was Kannan. Since she could not muster the courage to talk further, she simply went home. Later on, it transpired that my father's name at home was Kannan. His parents, siblings, and friends called him by this name.

Soon my parents got engaged. But prior to this, my grandparents put in a lot of effort to convince my mother for this alliance. They would take her for long walks and use this time to tell my mom that my dad was the most suitable groom for her. They influenced her in a gentle yet firm way by insisting that, 'Skin colour does not matter whereas the family background, culture and upbringing mattered the most.'

My grandparents kept reassuring my mother that she would be looked after well if she married Kannan! After long monologues by her parents, my mother finally agreed to marry my father, but only because of family pressure. She once told me, "I agreed to marry him because of the pressure, but I also thought if I didn't like him, I could get a divorce." Such thinking reflects her strength and courage even at a young age.

The time between engagement and wedding was about 4 months. Here, I must reveal that mom and dad came from very different cultures. Since my dad belonged to Chennai, the culture there was very different from that of Bangalore, the place where my mom was born and brought up. She was very romantic at heart and expected a birthday card and love messages but my dad was unaware of these things. Though she was a bit disappointed, she accepted their differences.

The wedding took place at Kamakshi temple Kanchipuram on February 23, 1973. My dad is a gem of a human being. He always loved and protected my mom from the word go and my mum dearly loved him. Both of them were strong individuals in their own way. Both worked in a bank. While my father worked in United Bank of India, my mom as mentioned earlier worked in RBI but did not accept any promotions to give stability to the family. My dad, on the other hand, scaled the career ladder and was constantly away from family due to frequent transfers. For nearly 10 years, mom took care of us mostly alone because work took my dad to various places like Odisha, Delhi, and Chennai. He could manage to visit us only once in two months and that too for a few days.

Slowly their relationship evolved in such a way that my dad became more nurturing while my mom took charge of home and made all decisions. Here, I need to stress on the fact that my mom never disobeyed my father. This was something which was not known to many. People outside often thought my mom was bossy and dad was quiet; it appeared as if my mom was dominating but the truth is they had their own special way of understanding each other.

Similarly, she shared a deep bond of love and understanding with her siblings. Being the eldest in the family, she doted on her younger siblings. My mom's brother Viswewaran, an engineer from Regional Engineering college and an IIM graduate who currently lives in the US and her sister Vidya, a doctor who lives in Canada adored and loved their elder sister dearly.

■

An Architect of Opportunity

At eighteen, she wrote the Reserve Bank of India exam which was very tough and got selected. That job became an anchor for the rest of her life. Her career path, however, was anything but simple. Working in a bank meant constant transfers and the tough choice of choosing between professional success vis-a-vis a balanced home life. Since my father was also a banker, whenever he moved to a new place, my mother would request for a transfer too so that the entire family could live together. As a child, I was quite unaware of the fact that each transfer meant starting as the junior-most employee. Her promotions and seniority got reset every time we moved to a new place. Yet she never grumbled. She willingly gave up promotions so that her children's education and welfare could always come first.

She always said, "My three children are my world, my job can never supersede them". She managed her work with sharp efficiency, finished her tasks early, and rushed home to take care of us. Her colleagues often said, 'Geetha is the most astute employee in our office who can quickly master new tasks and excel in multitasking also. We look up to her and aspire to be as efficient and productive like her'. For 27 years, she did everything - office work, housework, cooking, and parenting with little domestic help. In her professional life, she worked extensively in various departments like Foreign Exchange, Public Accounts Department, Security establishment etc. Exceptionally adaptable, she quickly mastered every department she worked in and performed efficiently in each. Even now, thinking about it fills me with awe. Her strength was her power. She showed me that strength isn't about physical might, but about emotional resilience and consistency.

My mother also had an amazing gift for managing finances. She planned every rupee, saved wisely, and never wasted anything. But she was not miserly - she was thoughtful. She believed that money had to serve a purpose: education, security, and service to others. She guided relatives to invest in land, securing bright futures for many beyond her immediate circle. She took extreme care and did extensive enquiries before recommending or purchasing a plot. Even to this day, many people remember her fondly saying, 'We enjoy living in our own home because of the efforts of Geetha amma. She had nothing to gain, yet she made it a mission to put a roof over our heads.'

In fact, her true genius shone in the domain of financial prudence and planning. From a young age, she made wise investments, scrutinizing housing society opportunities and always consulting others repeatedly to ensure good decisions. My mother used to save money and buy 1 gram gold every month from the government mint which was so handy during mine and my siblings' weddings. Her fierce attention to detail, her insistence on saving yet providing us top-tier education, instilled lessons that money must be respected, not squandered.

■

Guiding Her Children to Independence

As a hands-on mother, she had one clear vision - to raise independent, disciplined children. She always said, "Love without guidance spoils, guidance without love hardens. You must balance both." And she lived by that. She didn't pamper us endlessly but taught us to spend money wisely and believed that spending on yourself is really an investment in your own growth!

During our formative years, my mother crafted an environment that balanced warmth and structure. Her philosophy was simple: hand-hold, when necessary, admonish when needed, and, above all, stand as our pillar of support.

She also made sure our minds were well-fed. Vacations were never just for fun - they were journeys filled with learning, exploration, and gratitude. When my dad, as the eldest son, wanted to take his parents to Varanasi, my mom happily bore the cost of the flights for them while my father availed the leave facility concession from his bank which covered the flight expenses for us. My mom took good care of her in-laws during the trip. My paternal grandfather deeply admired my mom and adored her especially for her sharp financial wisdom, planning and support.

Education was central to her strategy for empowerment. She didn't force her children's paths but I am grateful for the fact that my mother was unwavering in her insistence on discipline and hard work. She monitored our studies, provided sharp counsel when marks dropped, and never shied away from criticism if it meant improvement. Rewards were earned, not given. Under her watch, we learned that work comes before comfort, and gratitude before pride. She wanted me and my siblings to grow into self-sufficient, kind, and strong adults. And she succeeded.

My sister and I became doctors while my younger brother became an engineer. But she never claimed credit. She said, "I only guided you; you walked the path." Still, all of us knew that every exam passed, every challenge overcome, carried her invisible hand behind it.

Coming back to our journey into the professional world, as we got busy in our respective careers, she neither took a back seat nor became totally intrusive. She remained mindfully engaged -a sounding board for doubts, a steadying hand during transitions, and a cheerleader for every accomplishment. She considered our marriages a sacred responsibility, ensuring we found stability and joy in our choices. Her role in my life became especially profound. When I started practicing as a gynaecologist, my mother once again became my pillar of strength. She took care of my children with the same love she showed me. She became their grandmother, teacher, and guide rolled into one. She narrated stories, set routines, and infused their young hearts with the same mix of joy and discipline that shaped me.

■

Strength Amidst Storms

Life presented my mother with more than her fair share of hardship. Like they say, even heroes face their battles. My mother's first battle came quite early in life. The loss of her youngest brother Sai who had a heart condition when she was just eight introduced her to sorrow prematurely. Later, every job transfer was another test of her endurance. Each transfer in her career was not merely a physical shift but an emotional upheaval - her years of service often went uncredited, promotions deferred, yet she bore this, steadfast, for the sake of her family. She continued to stay strong.

Physical health, too, was a source of trial. In 2000, after a major surgery, she slowed down physically but not mentally. Her spirit remained as vibrant as ever. In July 2017, she was diagnosed with Progressive Supranuclear Palsy (PSP). As a doctor and a daughter, I shed tears for many days. Having seen patients with this atypical Parkinson's, I could not imagine her slowly losing her independence and becoming bedridden.

Many might have succumbed to bitterness in the face of such news, but my mother refused to curse fate or dwell on her condition. From day one, she didn't let the illness win. She greeted each day with gratitude, never allowing the disease to define her. Through her words and behaviour, she radiated positivity that touched everyone. She taught us that illness can affect the body but never the spirit. Every time someone asked how she was, she smiled gently and said, **"I am fine."** That was her mantra till the very end.

Till the very end, dad was the best husband mom could ever have. Their journey together through time and trials showed that true love is about standing together through all struggles, not just about looks or wealth. It was indeed a love beyond differences. For me, theirs was a truly successful marriage in every sense of the word!

Another deep emotional blow came in the year 2020, when my grandmother passed away. After this loss my mother's health began to decline more rapidly. Though her health weakened, her heart stayed full of faith and love. Even when speech left her and movement became hard, she continued to bless everyone with her eyes and smile. Whenever we asked how she was, she continued to say, "I am fine," even though we could see she was getting weaker. That was her positive spirit. I used to call her every day and say, "I love you." She would always say back, "I love you too, Uma." Even now, I still hear her words in my heart whenever I think of her.

By late 2024, communication was reduced to gestures and fleeting eye contact. Yet, her presence at family gatherings, her quiet strength, continued to be the gravity around which her loved ones revolved.

■

A Legacy of Love and Lessons

My mother's life was a lesson in balance - discipline and kindness, strength and softness. She was deeply spiritual. She used to do fasting and prayer to Santhoshi Maa on Fridays. She visited temples quite often especially Siva, Sai Baba and Banashankari temple. She undertook all the pilgrimages to Badrinath, Kedarnath, Kashi and Rameshwaram.

Those who were sheltered under 'Geetha's wings' remember her with reverence. Her teachings were both practical and profound: plan wisely, respect elders, pray earnestly, and face every challenge head-on. She cared deeply for her parents, supporting her mother for eighteen years and orchestrating household rituals with meticulous devotion. Her commitment transcended family boundaries; she helped domestic workers arrange marriages, sponsored education for struggling students, and provided emotional lifelines to colleagues in distress-even saving a colleague who was contemplating suicide through compassionate candour and support.

As mentioned earlier, her handling of finances was legendary; she invested not only for her family, but also helped friends and relatives to invest, ensuring others benefited from her acumen. The societies she supported include Bharani Cooperative Housing Society, Ravi Cooperative Housing Society, Telecom Employees Society, RBE

Cooperative society etc. These societies were more than places to live; they were opportunities created for others to succeed. She generously gifted good land and property to me and my siblings, sharing everything equally. She also invested our earnings wisely with excellent returns.

■

Enduring Optimism and Final Farewell

To the very end, my mother's optimism was a force of nature. She greeted visitors with a smile, often muffled by her illness, yet radiant in her eyes. Her mornings began with prayer, her days structured around supporting her children and grandchildren, and her evenings with introspective gratitude.

Even after losing her voice, she never lost her will to communicate strength. When her final days came, she couldn't speak anymore, but her eyes still told stories. I held her hand, and she pressed mine firmly, as if passing a secret message: "Always remain strong, come what may." Those present at her bedside understood this was not a goodbye, but a passing of the torch - a reminder that hardship is not a barrier but a teacher, and that hope endures even when words cannot.

■

Geetha's Guiding Principles

Across five decades, my mother's life imparted lessons that resonate long after her passing. Her words and deeds offer a blueprint for navigating the complexities of modern life. She believed:

- "Let adversity be your teacher, not your master."
- "Live simply, give generously, plan wisely, and love deeply."
- "When you cannot run, walk. When you cannot walk, stand. But never give up."

Her mantra, "I am fine," continues to resonate in the hearts of all who knew her, a quiet reflection of her enduring courage.

■

The Ripple Effect

Geetha's children including yours truly feel blessed that we bear the spirit of her guidance in every accomplishment and in every step of our lives. Her rigorous standards, unwavering support, and steady counsel shaped not only our careers but our characters. We remember her evenings organizing studies, her gentle rebukes when deadlines were missed, and her pride in our achievements-each a testament to my mother's relentless pursuit of our independence.

Her grandchildren too recall the stories she told, the lessons she imparted through everyday actions, and the love she wrapped around them like a protective shield. Her presence in their formative years, especially her care during my demanding professional journey, ensured they grew up grounded, grateful, and inspired by her example.

Extended family and friends recall my mother's hospitality, her warmth at every festival, and the sense of welcome that filled her home. She organized every pooja with elaborate detail, reinforcing traditions while making space for new memories. Her guidance was widely sought, her patience admired, and her personal struggles received with empathetic hearts, as she never allowed her own difficulty to become a burden to others.

Her story continues through us -her children, her grandchildren, and everyone whose life she touched. Whenever I doubt myself, I think of her gentle smile and hear her steady voice inside me saying, "You will be fine." And then I know that I carry her courage within me.

■

Conclusion: A Life Well-Lived

Geetha Balasubramanian's life is a chronicle of quiet victories and indomitable resolve. Hers is a legacy not of wealth or status, but of enduring strength, wise stewardship, and unwavering love. Her journey reminds us that the most profound impact is created not by monumental feats, but by the daily choices to love, guide, and persevere. To all who seek inspiration, her story is both a map and a lighthouse, illuminating the path of hope and unconditional support.

As her children, grandchildren, and friends continue on their paths, the echo of Geetha's life remains- a testament that true greatness is born of patience, hard work, and a heart that refuses to surrender, even in the face of the greatest adversity.

To me and everyone who knew her, my mother was much more than just a mother, wife, friend or a working woman. She was the person we leaned on, the one who helped us grow stronger and kinder, and whose strength set an example I try to follow each and every day.

■

AFTERWORD

As I look back on my journey, I realize that everything I am today I owe to my parents, most profoundly, to my mother. Every achievement, every milestone in my medical career - from M.B.B.S to D.G.O, MRCGP, MRCOG, DFSRH, and a postgraduate degree in Healthcare Leadership bears her invisible signature. Her guidance shaped not only my professional path but the very person I have become.

My mother's practical wisdom and steadfast discipline transformed me from a sensitive child into a resilient adult. Her tough love taught me to face life's challenges head-on, turning moments of struggle into stepping stones for growth. She never let me fall; instead, she stood beside me, lifting me through every hurdle, from academic battles to the uncertainties of living abroad.

The first turning point in my life came when I was around twelve years old. I was an extremely sensitive child unable to handle even the smallest criticism. Brought up by my grandparents, protected and pampered, I led a very sheltered life. When my parents moved to Bangalore, I went to live with them. My mother was a very practical and disciplined woman, and she couldn't bear to see me cry over every little thing.

One day, after yet another tearful episode, she told my father firmly, "I am going to fix this. Whatever happens, don't open the door even if she cries." Then she sat me down and said patiently, "You can't cry for every silly thing. Talk it out but don't cry." Being stubborn and emotional, I cried even louder. That's when she was very firm with me. At that moment, I had to decide whether I would remain the same overly sensitive child or become stronger. I chose strength. Looking back, I realized that moment changed me forever. I toughened up, learned to face life headon and, over the years, my mum became my best friend.

The second turning point came when I got admission to Mysore Medical College for my M.B.B.S. I had to stay in a hostel, which I absolutely hated. My dream had always been to study engineering at University Visvesvaraya College of Engineering (UVCE) and I had even secured a seat there. I told my parents that unless I got a transfer to Bangalore Medical College, I would quit medicine altogether. My mom didn't argue or scold me. Instead, she took action. She literally stood outside Bangalore Medical College on admission day, asking every student who walked by if they wanted a mutual transfer to Mysore. The odds of finding someone were almost zero, but her determination was unshakable. Miraculously, she found a girl who wanted to study in Mysore and that's how I ended up in Bangalore Medical College, continuing my medical journey. That persistence of hers changed my destiny.

When I first came to the UK, I stayed in a student accommodation in East Ham and to my horror, it was infested with rats. Terrified, I called my parents in tears and told them I wanted to return to India immediately. My dad said I could come back the very next day, but my mum listened quietly and said, "There are eight other girls living with you, so you will be fine. Just stay for a week. If you still feel miserable, come back after that." I agreed reluctantly. The next day, I went to a local hospital, got a clinical attachment, and discovered a workplace culture I loved. When she asked a week later if I was coming home, I laughed and said, "Why would I? It's so good here." Had it not been for her calm patience, I might have returned and my life would have been entirely different.

During my early days in the UK, I often felt lonely and homesick. My mother told me, "Celebrate every festival, cook your favourite dishes, and keep our traditions alive." Her advice kept me connected to my roots, my culture, and my sense of self. Even miles away, she made sure our heritage lived on through me.

Life threw me another challenge when I began preparing for my MRCOG exams. I had my son then and couldn't focus on studying. I failed my first attempt. But my mother, ever my pillar, told me to leave my son with her for a year so I could focus fully on the exam. Thanks to her selflessness, I passed with flying colours. Later, when I took my MRCGP exam, I left my daughter with my parents for a year too and again, I succeeded. Every degree I have earned has my parents' sacrifices woven into it. Her wisdom didn't stop at academics or family. She also guided me financially.

I must also mention that she had an exquisite taste in clothes and jewellery; many of her friends sought her advice and help for selecting jewellery and dresses.Every saree and ornament I own has her touch in it.

Every mother inspires her child, but mine lived every lesson she taught me. She built my foundation, moulded my strength, and guided my journey at every crossroads. If I stand tall today, it's because she never let me fall.

Her persistence in securing my education, her thoughtful guidance through life's milestones like marriage, and her sacrifices for my success are woven into every accomplishment I hold dear. Even when I was continents away, it was her steady voice and enduring support that kept me connected to my roots, my culture, and my identity.

More than the grand gestures, it was her countless small acts like investing in our future, managing the home front, nurturing traditions that built the foundation of my life.

This memoir is a tribute to her strength, wisdom, and love. While the pages may end here, her influence continues to inspire every step I take.

I am sure my readers would agree that her life story has the power to ignite hope, courage and transform many lives!

This book is also dedicated to my father, a true gem of a human being. His kindness, fairness, and unwavering love have been the steady foundation of our family. Everything my mother achieved in her life was made possible by his constant support and encouragement.

Through our most challenging moments, he remained calm, patient, and steadfast, carrying out his responsibilities without ever seeking praise or reward. He treats every person with equal dignity, and his gentle strength has touched all who know him.

As the most devoted caregiver my mother could have wished for, we are certain that no one could have cared for her as he did. He never once complained about the difficulties; instead, he simply did his very best, giving everything he had to look after her, showing his love through every thoughtful act of care.

He walks like a king and from him, I have learned patience, grace, and the deep importance of bringing people together in all that I do.

■

In Loving Memory of Geetha- Through my Father's Eyes

I met many girls before I met Geetha, but I found them to be passive and never really liked any of them. But in October 1972, the moment I saw Geetha I instantly liked her. I was drawn to her sharp, expressive eyes and the confidence in her voice. With my father and family beside me, and with God's blessings, our marriage took place in February 1973. She was only twenty-two: young, beautiful, and full of grace.

Geetha loved films and film songs, especially Hindi songs. She loved reading novels. I was more into sports, chess, cricket, and social work, so our interests differed significantly. Yet we complemented each other in every way. Although she did not know much cooking when we married, she learned cooking with love and patience as I liked tasty food. Though she was a poor eater herself, she mastered the art of preparing delicious dishes. She experimented with sweets and also made wonderful Andhra avakkai pickles, which I enjoyed.

She had a natural sense of beauty. Her hairstyles, elegance, and the composure she carried in her career made her stand out. She carried a unique grace in her career, marked by versatility and composure. One day, when I visited the Hyderabad branch of the Reserve Bank of India where she worked alongside about 300 women, I asked an officer where I could find Geetha. He replied, 'Oh, you're looking for the beauty of the office.' I felt very happy to hear this.

Family was everything to her. For me, my office was everything. Despite these differences, we had a very successful marriage because of her cooperation, patience, and countless sacrifices. She bore the difficulties of all my transfers without once complaining, though she missed my company dearly. Even when I was physically present, I had to work on Sundays too due to heavy workload. She accepted all this quietly.

She loved her job, but when I was transferred to Ranchi in 1974, where there was no RBI branch for her, she prepared herself to leave the job for my sake- an immense sacrifice indeed. Thankfully, the people in my head office knew the value of RBI job and helped me. They did not want her to resign, and within ten months, I was transferred to Hyderabad so that she could continue.

Geetha kept every record and every small paper safely including tiny prescription slips. This habit later helped me greatly when I had to convince the RBI management to transfer her to Hyderabad, as she was repeatedly falling ill in the coastal climate of Chennai.

Her memory was remarkable. She could recall phone numbers of relatives and friends effortlessly. If I asked for an old record, she would find it in minutes, as though she had kept it only yesterday. She had leadership qualities too. In NCC, where everyone joins as a cadet and only a very few become Under Officers, she rose to become one of those few.

Her financial foresight was extraordinary. In 1980 she invested ₹72,000 in Malleswaram Society. After twenty years, when allotment did not take place despite the secretary's assurances, she withdrew the money in 2002. Seven or eight years later, the society had no money left to repay anyone. Many who trusted the society suffered losses but she had foreseen the risk.

In another case, allotment came but legal complications arose for thirty-six people, including us. In 2016, Geetha wrote a letter requesting an alternate site, even though the allotted one was very good. The secretary kept assuring us it would be resolved, but she insisted on the alternative. Eight years later, the alternate site was granted. Many others are still waiting. Her ability to sense what would happen in the future was extraordinary.

Like any human being, she had her faults. But those who treated her well were treated even better by her. She always went above and beyond for people who were good to her. Those who did not treat her well were simply ignored.She could not stand dishonesty or lies and never hesitated to show her anger toward it. She had many reasons for every decision she took; she always weighed things carefully, though few understood her depth.

She also planned our travels with great precision. After my retirement, we travelled together to the UK, Singapore, Malaysia, China, Hong Kong, Macau, Dubai, Abu Dhabi, Switzerland, Italy, France, and Austria. She organized everything with her RBI colleagues, always ensuring that the trips were comfortable and reasonably priced.

She made countless sacrifices for me, and kept our family happy. Through her financial wisdom, she left us assets and security even after her passing. I miss her deeply.

Today, when I think of her, I see how much she shaped our life with her strength, intelligence, care, and vision. Her memory lives on in everything she did.... for us, our home, and everyone she loved.

And I cherish her forever.

■

Dr. Sivaraman

Geetha's son-in-law and Uma's husband

I first met Mami (mother-in-law in Tamil) in Chennai around 2003. My first impression of her was that she was a task-driven and focused person living entirely for her family. She was an eye opener for us in terms of smart investment. But initially, I overlooked this aspect. But over the years, I realized that her professional expertise and upbringing played a significant role in her insight into finance. Today, we continue to benefit from some of the investments she advised us on, and I am deeply grateful to her for her wisdom and guidance.

Above all, she was a great confidence booster, infusing positivity and motivation to overcome life's hurdles, no matter the challenges. Her inspiration powered our growth and well-being. May her soul rest in peace and always bless us, take us though the right path and direct us through the right way to achieve peace for everybody.

■

Arun Rajamani

Geetha's Son-in-law

My interactions with Mami were always warm and good fun. She had a lovely though dry sense of humour.She brought a joie de vivre to the family that would be truly missed.

■

Nithya

Daughter-in-law

One of my most memorable experiences took place on February 21, 2004, when we were traveling from Salem to Bangalore for my engagement. Around 7:30 PM, near the erstwhile Jewels De Paragon on M.G. Road, our car accidentally brushed against another vehicle. The young couple in the other car stopped us and began arguing with our driver, who could not communicate well in the local language. My father had already gone ahead in an auto rickshaw to locate The Malleswaram Club (Choultry), leaving us momentarily stranded.

We immediately called my mother-in-law for help and she arrived within minutes. She came with the Chief of RBI Security, a military captain, and a few influential friends. With a no-nonsense approach and remarkable clarity, she quickly resolved the situation.

That evening perfectly reflected what I have always admired about her: her thorough preparation, deep thought, stunning efficiency, and her ability to read people and situations instantly, always planning two steps ahead. Her strength and foresight remain a lasting inspiration to me.

■

Srivatsa

Geetha's grandson & Uma's son

My grandmother was an intensely motivated and deeply resilient woman whose presence continues to shape my sense of purpose and determination. She lived her life with a rare combination of discipline, clarity, and heartfelt devotion, and she passed those values on to me with every conversation we shared. From a young age, she always urged me to stay focused and study well, reminding me that education was not just a pathway to success but a responsibility I owed to myself and to the future she so passionately envisioned for me. Her words were never harsh, instead they carried a gentle firmness that made me want to strive harder, to honour her belief in my abilities. She prayed for me tirelessly, each prayer a quiet expression of her hopes, her love, and her unwavering faith that I would one day achieve everything she dreamed for me.

Her strength extended far beyond emotional encouragement; she possessed an extraordinary bravery that guided the way she lived and made decisions. She was remarkably wise with money, always thinking ahead, saving with intention, and investing in land when others hesitated. These choices reflected not only her intelligence but also her determination to build something lasting for the generations that would follow her. She faced challenges with a calm resolve, turning difficult moments into opportunities to demonstrate her courage and foresight.

Yet, above all the qualities that made her so remarkable, it was her passion for my success that remains most vivid in my memory. She celebrated every achievement, no matter how small, and reminded me that my journey did not end with a degree; she envisioned me growing, thriving, and shaping a meaningful life. Her faith in me became a driving force behind my ambitions, and even now, her words and prayers feel like a steady hand guiding me forward.

■

Sneha

granddaughter & Uma's daughter

When I was three years old, my grandmother became like a true mother to me during the ten months I lived with her. That time shaped me deeply, and I still carry its lessons today. She taught me so much, she was someone I truly admired. Shopping was one of our shared joys, and thanks to her impeccable taste, I was always the best dressed girl when I was in India. Even now, the majority of my Indian clothes were chosen by her, a lasting reminder of our shared passion. I deeply admired her goal-oriented mindset. The way she carried herself with her head held high, radiating an aura of authority, strength, and confidence is a recollection that I will cherish and emulate.

She was remarkably intelligent, smart, and sharp, with an exceptional judgement of people. One memory that remains vivid in my mind is watching her calculate the expenses for a function; despite living with Parkinson's. Her mental maths was quicker and more accurate than all of ours, and she effortlessly outpaced us. It left me astonished. She loved brushing my hair, and the tresses of others as well, and this simple, tender habit is one I have inherited from her.

I will continue learning from her throughout my life. I love her deeply, and she will forever live in our hearts. I admired her immeasurably, especially for the strength she showed while facing the daily challenges of Parkinson's, which affected her ability to speak, walk, eat, and swallow. Yet every time I called and asked, "How are you?" she always said up until the very day she passed, "I'm fine." Her bravery in those moments is something I can never forget.

■

Akashpranav

grandson & Vijay's son

My vivid memory of my beloved grandmother is a collection of incidents that has left an indelible impression on me and have taught me many aspects of successful living. I remember how she used to travel to Pune with my beloved grandfather. She would have a daily plan of the places she wanted to visit. She would disclose 2 places but end up showing us 4 places, this taught me the importance of doing your homework and planning meticulously. Her high energy was a sheer pleasure to watch. I saw her and learnt the importance of curiosity and initiative.

She would build an excellent rapport with the driver, co-travellers and even strangers. They often shared valuable information with her, which taught me the importance of building strong relationships-something possible only when one is genuine and truly adds value to others. Her generosity and willingness to give endeared her to everyone.

I learnt the power of positivity and grace from her. Even at the peak of her illness, she always said she was fine. I was fortunate to meet her every single day, and I will forever cherish her memory, the wonderful person she was, and the priceless lessons I learnt from our interactions.

■

Aadhithya

grandson & Vijay's son

My grandmother was an exceptionally sharp and skilful woman whose strength and spirit inspired everyone around her, even as she bravely battled PSP. A wonderful listener, I will never forget the time she patiently listened to me describe my Australia trip for half an hour. Her ability to plan and execute with precision was remarkable.

I was blessed to spend time with her every single day over the past three years. Her warmth, wisdom, and determined spirit continue to live on in our hearts and memories forever.

■

Aditi

granddaughter & Meena's daughter

Paati (grandmother in Tamil) was an exceptional human being with a great capacity for kindness and generosity. She was always there for me whenever I needed her. Her honesty was what touched me. Paati was not one to mince her words but rather told it as it was. I will never forget her honesty and dogmatic behaviour, and it is something I continue to take inspiration from.

■

Ananth

Grandson & Meena's son

My grandmother was kind and caring. My lasting memory of her is captured in the phrase E pluribus unum - Latin for 'Out of many, one.' From many diverse individuals, she created one loving family.

Sudha Chandraseker

Geetha's cousin

Geetha, my cousin sister, has left a void in the hearts of several people, for she was a wonderful soul who had touched the lives of many relatives and friends.

I remember her as a teenager when she had visited my parental home in Coonoor along with my uncle. My semester exams were on at that time. She was very considerate and asked me to go ahead with my exam preparations. I felt bad that I could not entertain her but she was very sportive and put me at ease. That is the Geetha I knew.

Whenever we happened to visit Bangalore, I used to call her. Immediately, she would say, "Saapida va" (come for lunch in Tamil). Such was her hospitality. She and my brother-in-law welcomed us warmly and treated us to virundu saapadu! (a big feast with an array of dishes)

We often spoke at length on a variety of subjects, and every visit with her remains a cherished memory. I deeply admire her for being a loving and capable mother to three wonderful children and a devoted wife. She balanced her career and family life with remarkable grace and efficiency. I truly cherished every conversation we shared over the phone in recent times. Your memory, Geetha, will remain with us forever.

■

Sridevi

Uma's cousin-Geetha's sister's daughter

Geethamma, as I fondly called her, was deeply affectionate toward me. I remember her taking us to the magic show at the Reserve Bank premises and subsequently treating us to ghee rice. She also took us on delightful outings - to Ulsoor lake and Muthyala Maduvu falls where we even enjoyed an elephant ride.

I can still picture her sleeping on the sofa in the living room, calling out in annoyance whenever we tiptoed past the kitchen and accidentally woke her. She was such a light sleeper! Geethamma also loved shopping; I can still hear her cheerful voice saying, 'Show me the latest!' wherever she went.

■

Geetha

Geetha and Balu Marriage photo 1973

Geetha and Balu Reception photo 1973

Geetha and Balu in Hyderabad with Vijay and Meena 1980

Geetha's parents 60th Birthday celebration

Geetha Balu with Arun, Meena , Aditi

Geetha with her mother on her 80th birthday

Balu 70th birthday with family

Geetha with mum, daughter and granddaughter- 4 generations

Geetha with Balu in Spalding UK 2019 (1)

Geetha Balu with grandchidren 61st birthday

Srivatsa Upanayanam 2017

Akaashpranav upanayanam

Aadhithya upanayanam 2023

Balasubramaniam Sadhabishekam 80th birthday with family

Picture drawn by grandson Akashpranav